Key S

Science

Practice Test Booklet

Contents

Author
Tricia Young

Letts
EDUCATIONAL

The test questions, answers and marking advice contained in this publication are based upon the official test materials provided to schools, but do not reproduce those tests exactly. The official tests are supported by administrative and other guidance for teachers to use in setting the tests, marking them, and interpreting their results. The results your pupils achieve in taking the tests in this pack may not be the same as they achieve in the official tests.

First published 1996
New editions 1997, 1998
This edition 1999
Reprinted 2000, 2001

Letts Educational, 414 Chiswick High Road, London W4 5TF
Tel. 020 8996 3333
Fax 020 8742 8390

Author: Tricia Young

Editorial, design and production by Hart McLeod, Cambridge

British Library Cataloguing-in-Publication Data
A CIP record for this book is available from the British Library

ISBN 1 84085 330 1

Printed in Great Britain by Ashford Colour Press

Letts Educational, a division of Granada Learning Ltd. Part of the Granada Media Group.

Science A

Test A Levels 3–5

First Name:

____

Last Name:

____

School:

____

Instructions

Read all the words carefully. Look at the diagrams or pictures, which are there to help you.

The questions for you to answer are in grey boxes.

For example:

Complete these sentences.

Look for the ✎ to show you where to write your answer.

Remember to explain your answers if you are asked to do so.

GOOD LUCK!

Test A Levels 3–5

marks

1 Lighting up

Katy wanted to put lights in her dolls' house. She tried to build a circuit so that she could make the bedroom light work on its own, or make the living room light work on its own, or make both lights work at the same time.

a **Which of these circuits should she set up? Circle the correct letter.**

A

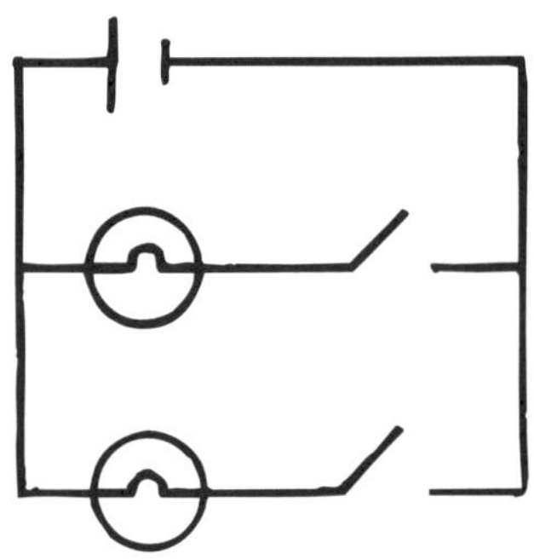

B

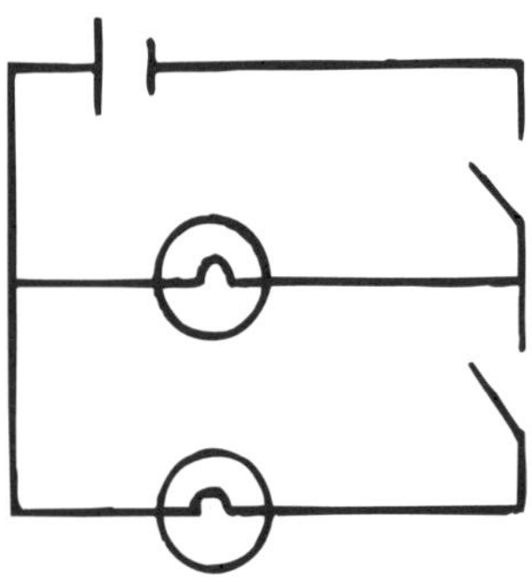

C

1

b When she came to wire the house she had no wire. marks

Which of the following could she use? Tick two.

foil		☑	string		☐
sticky tape		☐	straws		☐
paper clips		☑			

2

c **Explain your answer.**

because metal is a good conducter

1

d **What would happen to the lights if Katy used two batteries instead of one?**

the lights would be brighter.

1

e **As well as light, what else does the light bulb produce?**

electricity

1

2 Changing materials

marks

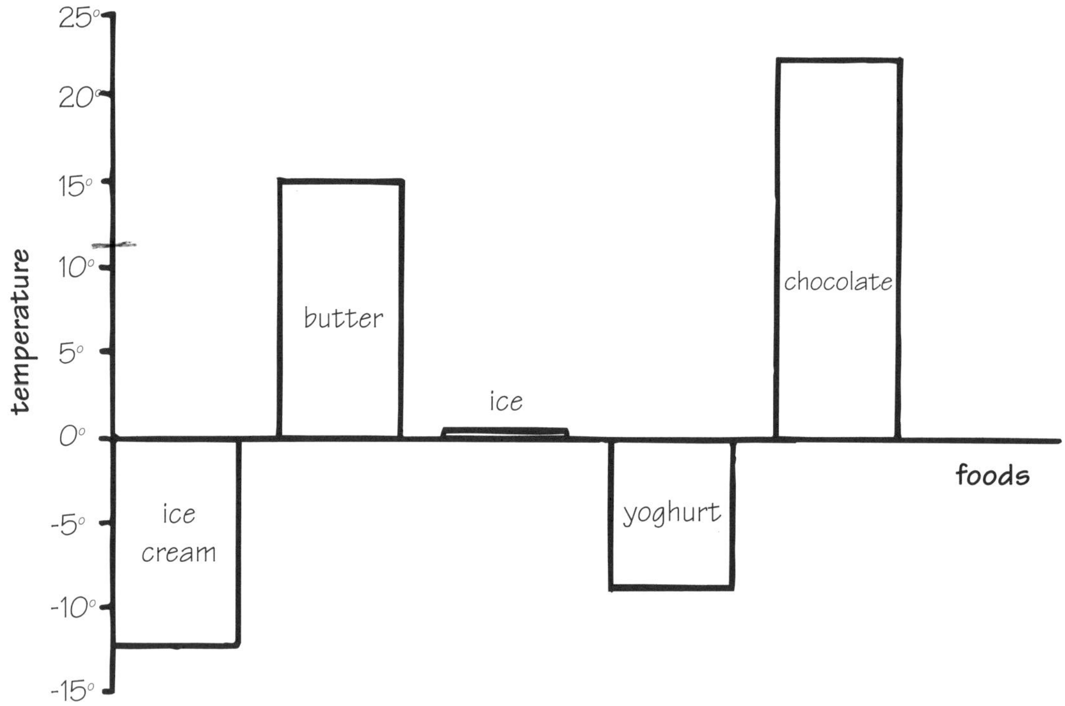

This bar chart shows the temperature at which some foods start to melt.

a **Which food melts at the highest temperature?**

chocolate

1

b The temperature in the kitchen is about 11°C.

Which foods should be kept in the fridge or freezer so that they stay solid?

ice cream

2

c I want to take a carton of ice-cream on a picnic. marks

Which is the best way to pack it so that it does not melt? Tick the correct answer.

Wrap it in newspaper in a plastic bag	✓
Put it in a biscuit tin	
Wrap it in newspaper in a paper bag	
Put it in a glass jar in a plastic bag	

1

d **Explain your answer.**

the newsPaper would help cool the ice cream down if the sun is on it.

2

3 Healthy eating

marks

a **Explain why too much sugar is bad for our teeth.**

Sugar is bad because it rots them

1

b A healthy diet consists of:

Carbohydrate	Protein	Fat	Vitamins
cream	orange	sweets	bread
beans	lettuce	peanut butter	egg

4

Write these foods in the correct boxes above.

sweets bread beans orange

egg cream peanut butter lettuce

marks

4 Forces

Ian and Rowan measured how far their bikes went with one turn of the pedals as they cycled along a flat path. They tested different gears.

Here is a table of their results.

Gear	Distance in cm
1	180
2	213
3	297
4	
5	402

a **What is the pattern between gear and distance? Put in a word to make the sentence true.**

The lower the gear the ___Slower___ the distance the bike travelled.

1

b **Predict the distance the bike would travel in 4th gear.**

___100___ cm

1

c They cycled up a steep hill. It took a lot of effort. **marks**

What was the force which made cycling more difficult?

friction

1

d **Draw an arrow on the diagram to show which way the force acts.**

1

e At the top of the hill they freewheeled downhill until they stopped.

What was the force which caused them to stop?

friction

1

f **Draw an arrow on the diagram to show which way the force acts.**

marks

1

g **Explain why pulling on the brakes makes the bike slow down.**

the friction of the tyres rubbing on a hot surface causes them to slow down.

1

5 Rocks and Soil

marks

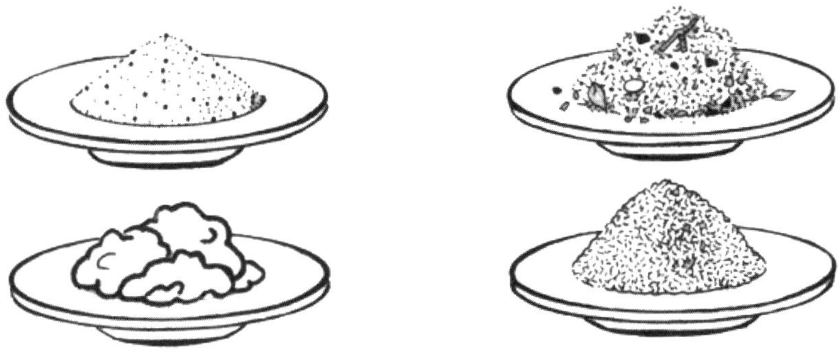

Eddy put 200g of each of the different types of soil into foil dishes and heated them in the oven at 120°C for an hour. When they had cooled he measured the mass of the soils. Here are his results.

Soil	Mass
sand	160g
clay	97g
garden soil	132g
compost	115g

a **What happened to make the mass of each soil sample change?**

hedid it for over an hour.

1

b **Explain why the mass of the clay changed the most.**

because it's more sloggy.

1

marks

Here is a graph showing how the mass of the clay changed.

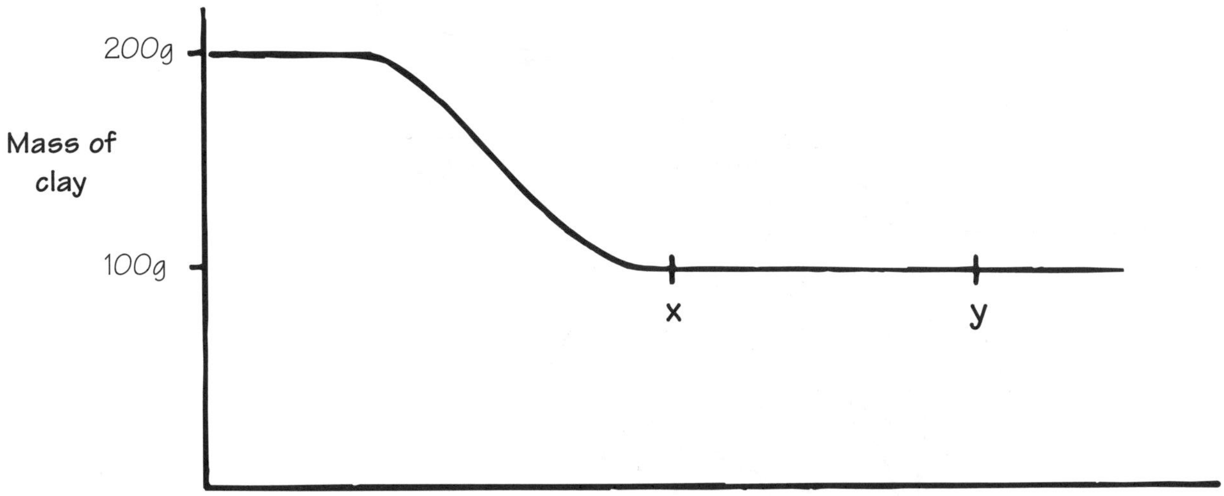

c **What happened to the mass between x and y?**

nothing

1

d **Explain your answer.**

it the line is just going straight

1

marks

6 Ourselves

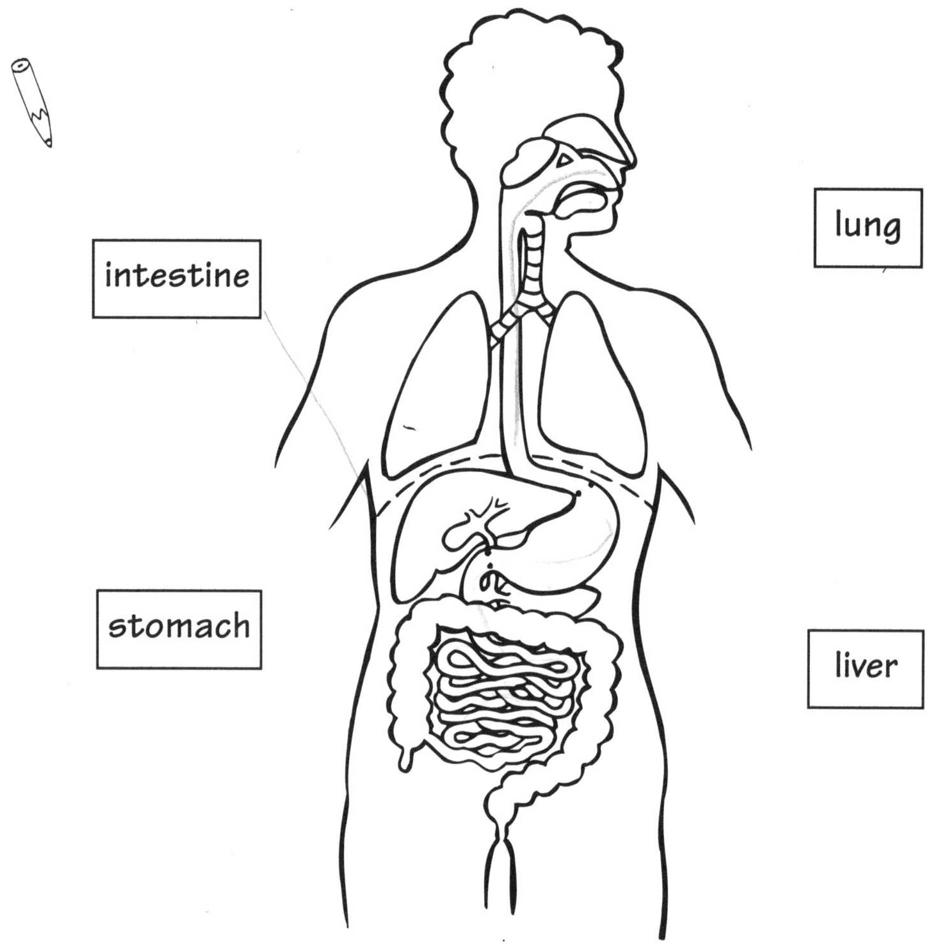

a **Draw a line from each box to the correct part of the body.** 4

b **Draw a line from the mouth to the stomach to show the way food travels.** 1

marks

7 Light

a **Draw a line from each object to the correct description.**

cardboard

tissue

transparent

milk bottle

key

opaque

net curtain

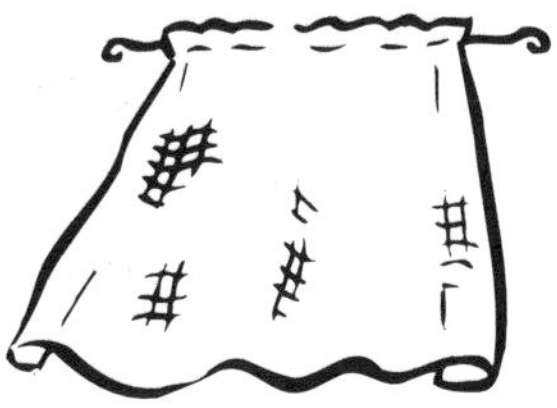

translucent

window

3

marks

b Hardeep looked at three spoons. One was made from steel, another from plastic and another from wood.

Explain why she could only see herself in the metal spoon.

____

____

____ 1

c She looked at an image of herself in a mirror.

Draw three arrows on the diagram to show how she could see herself.

2

8 Plant growth

marks

Sue and James planted some cress and mustard seeds. Each day they measured the height of the seedlings and worked out the average. They drew a graph of their results.

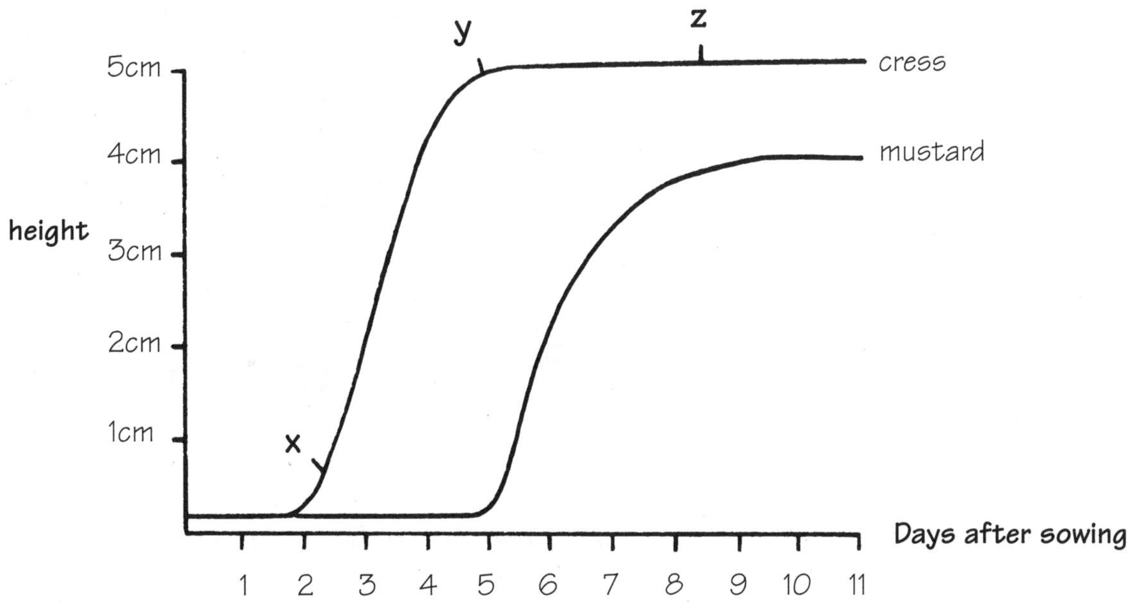

a **After how many days did the mustard germinate?**

____ 1

b **What happened to the cress between x and y?**

____ 1

c **What happened to the cress between y and z?**

____ 1

marks

d Name <u>two</u> things that seeds need in order to germinate.

____ 2

e Name <u>two</u> things that plants need in order to grow.

____ 2

Science B

Test B Levels 3–5

First Name:

Last Name:

School:

Instructions

Read all the words carefully. Look at the diagrams or pictures, which are there to help you.

The questions for you to answer are in grey boxes.

For example:

Complete these sentences.

Look for the pencil to show you where to write your answer.

Remember to explain your answers if you are asked to do so.

GOOD LUCK!

marks

1 Hardness

shell   iron nail   slate   chalk   stone

a Sally did an experiment to find out how hard some materials were. She tried to scratch one material with another.
Here is what she found out:

The shell scratched the stone and slate.

The iron nail scratched all the other materials.

The slate did not scratch the stone.

Everything scratched the chalk.

Put the materials in order of hardness.
Start with the hardest material.

_____________________ hardest

____

____

____

_____________________ softest

3

marks

b **Why do glass cutters use tiny diamonds as tools?**

1

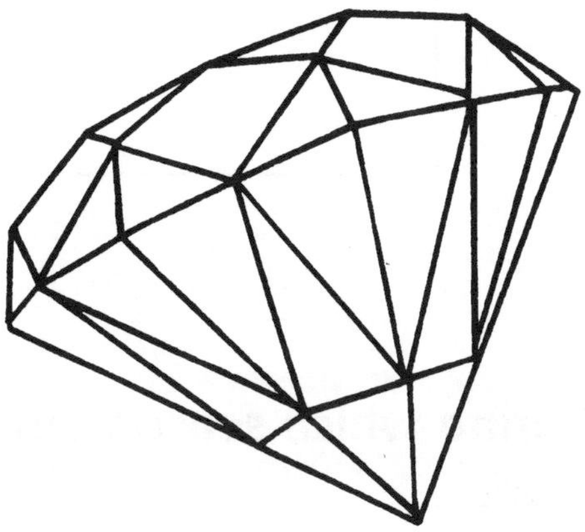

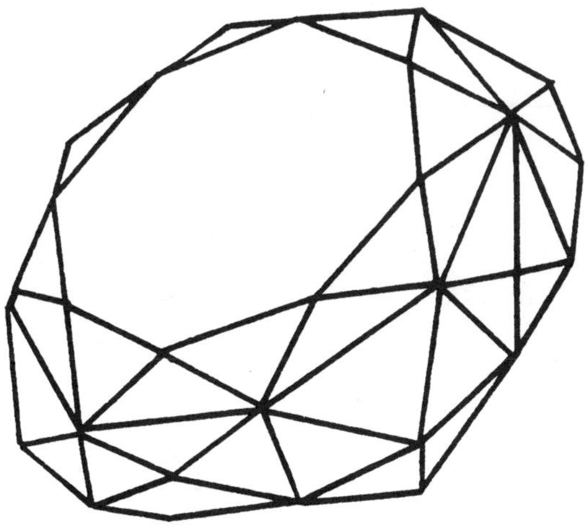

marks

2 Earth

A Year 6 class in Sheffield calculated the length of daylight over one month in the year.

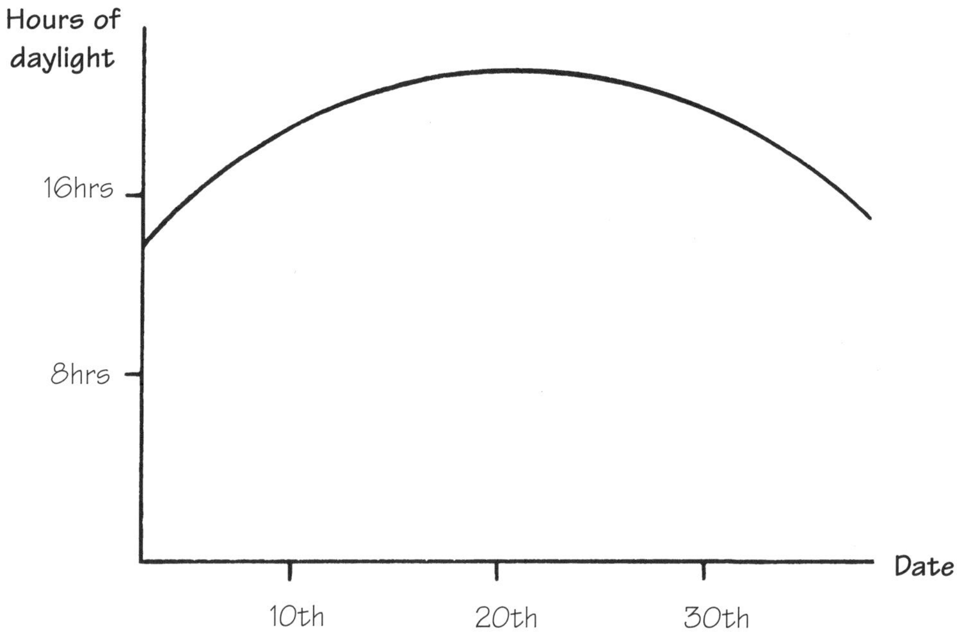

a **During which season did the children carry out the work?**

____ 1

b **Explain your answer.**

____

____

____ 1

marks

c **Draw on the graph the shape of the graph if the same investigation had been carried out in winter.**

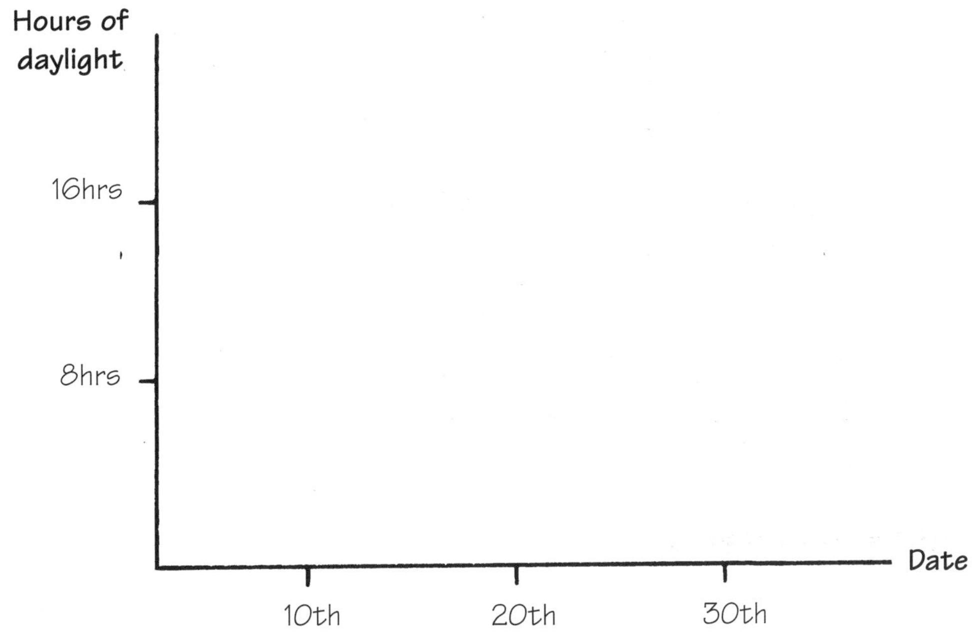

2

d **How long is a lunar month?**

☐ days

1

marks

3 Changing water

Alice left a jar of water without a lid on the window sill. Every morning she measured how much water was left. By the end of the week there was no more water left in the jar.

a **Where did the water go?**

____

____

1

Here is a graph of the amount of water in the jar each day.

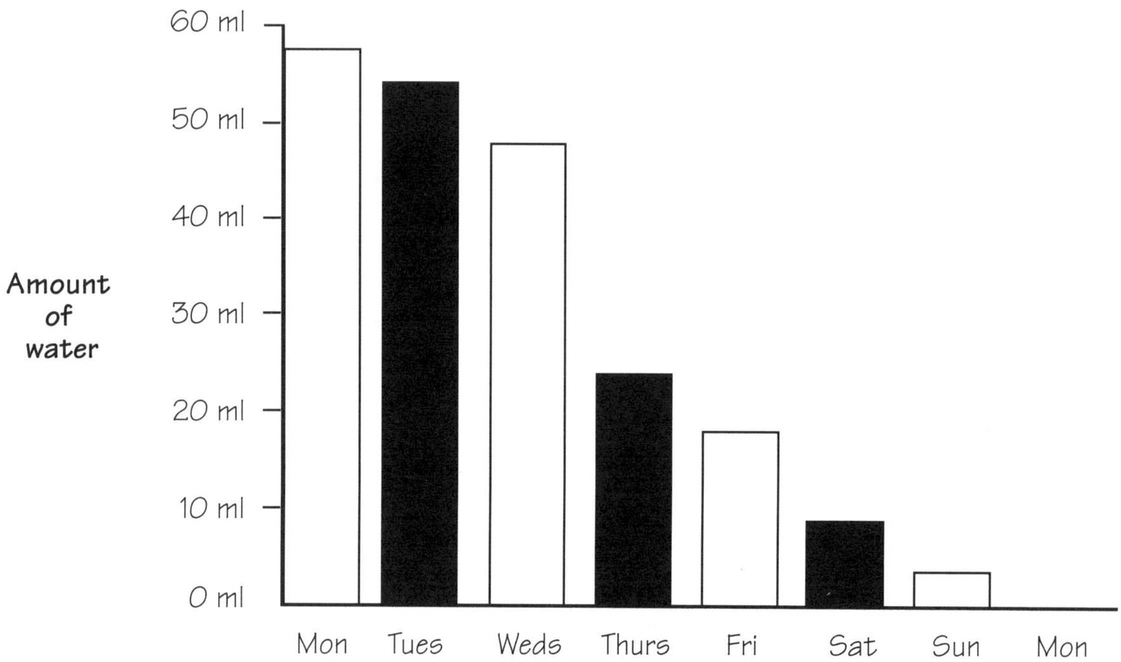

marks

b Look at the graph on page 24.

During which day did the amount of water in the jar drop the most?

____ 1

c **Give <u>two</u> reasons why this might have happened.**

____

____

____

____ 2

d **What could Alice have done to make sure that the water stayed in the jar?**

____

____

____

____ 1

marks

4 Feathers

Here is a diagram of a feather.

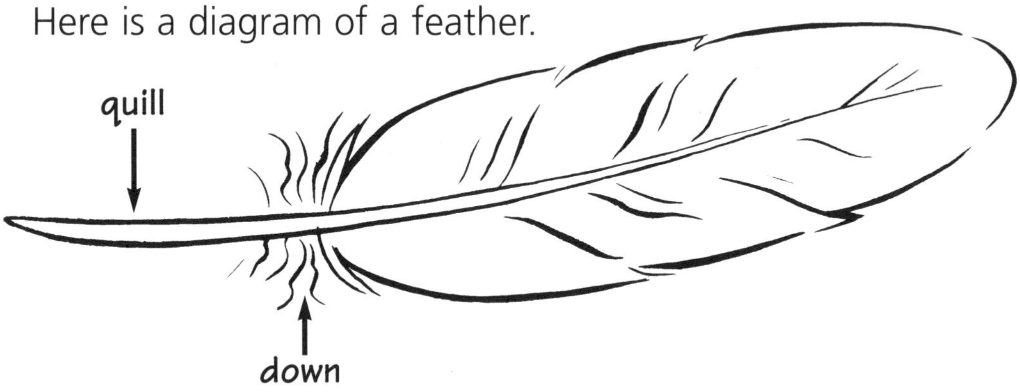

a **Give <u>one</u> reason why the quill is hollow.**

____ 1

b **What is the purpose of the tuft or down?**

____

____ 1

c **Write <u>two</u> things the feather protects the bird from.**

____

____ 2

d **Why do some birds have bright feathers?**

____

____

____ 1

marks

e **Why do some birds have dull feathers?**

____

____

____ 1

f **Tick <u>three</u> sentences that are true for all birds and fish.**

All are animals ☐

All need oxygen to breathe ☐

All have teeth ☐

All lay eggs ☐

All have scales ☐

All are herbivores ☐ 3

5 Small animals

a **Draw a line from each box to the correct part of the body.** 4

b **Explain why a spider is not an insect.**

____

____

____ 1

marks

c **Number the pictures to show the correct order of the life cycle of a butterfly.**

butterfly ☐

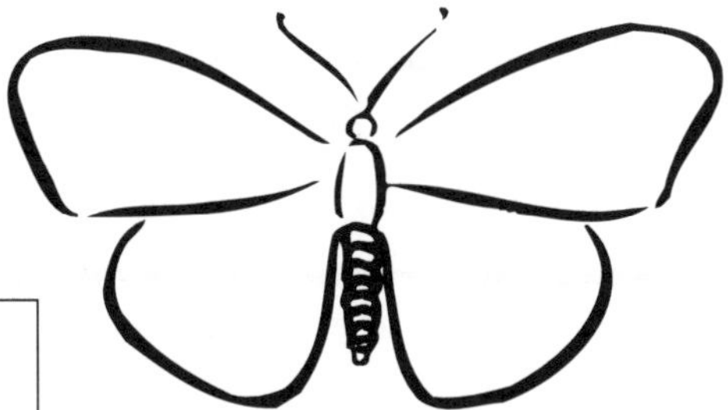

caterpillar ☐

eggs 1

pupa ☐

1

6 marks

Sound

Ainsley looked inside a piano. He saw many wires of a differing length and thickness. Each wire made a different note when struck. Here are four wires which might be found in a piano.

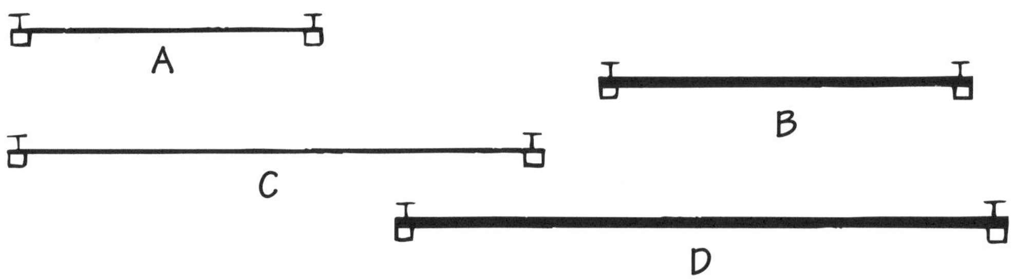

a **Which wire would produce the lowest note when struck?**

____

1

b **David blew through a straw to make a note. He then cut off half the length and blew through it again. How did the sound change?**

____

____

1

c **Explain why we cannot hear what is happening on the Sun but we can see it.**

____

____

____

2

marks

d David and Ainsley talked to each other on a string telephone.

What was the purpose of the string?

____

____

____

____

1

7 Separating mixtures

marks

Here are some ways Ibrahim used to separate mixtures.

Mixing with water and filtering

Sieving

Allowing it to stand

Using a magnet

a **Which way did he use to separate a mixture of sand and salt?**

____ 1

Explain why he chose this method.

____

____

____ 1

marks

b **Which way did he use to separate a mixture of oil and water?**

______________________________ 1

Explain why he chose this method.

____

____

____

______________________________ 1

c **Which way did he use to separate a mixture of sand and gravel?**

______________________________ 1

Explain why he chose this method.

____

____

____

______________________________ 1

marks

d **Which way did he use to separate the different parts of topsoil?**

____________________ 1

Explain why he chose this method.

____

____

____________________ 1

e **Which way did he use to separate a mixture of pins and matchsticks?**

____________________ 1

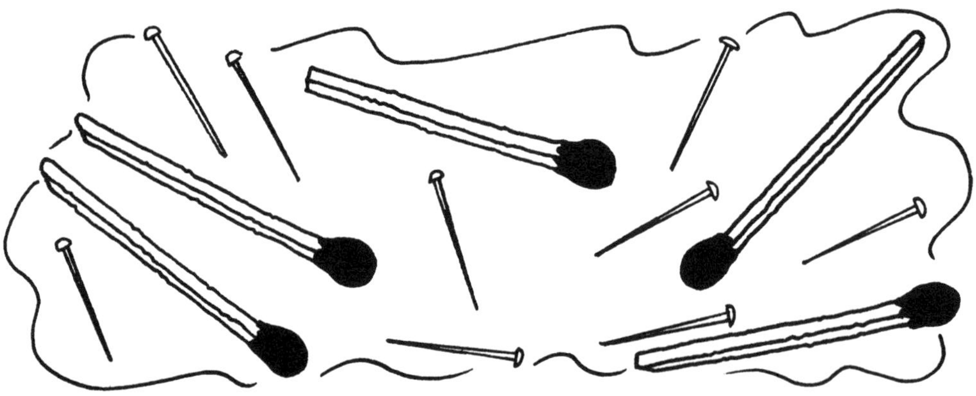

Explain why he chose this method.

____

____

____

____________________ 1

Resource Sheets

The following pages contain diagrams and activities for you to practise labelling, which you can keep as handy revision notes for your tests.

There is also a glossary on page 46 to help you revise and remember some of the more difficult science words and phrases you may need.

Resource Sheets

Letts KS2 Revision Notes for Science provide further help and are in full colour, providing all the essential information required for the KS2 National Tests in May.

marks

Label the skeleton

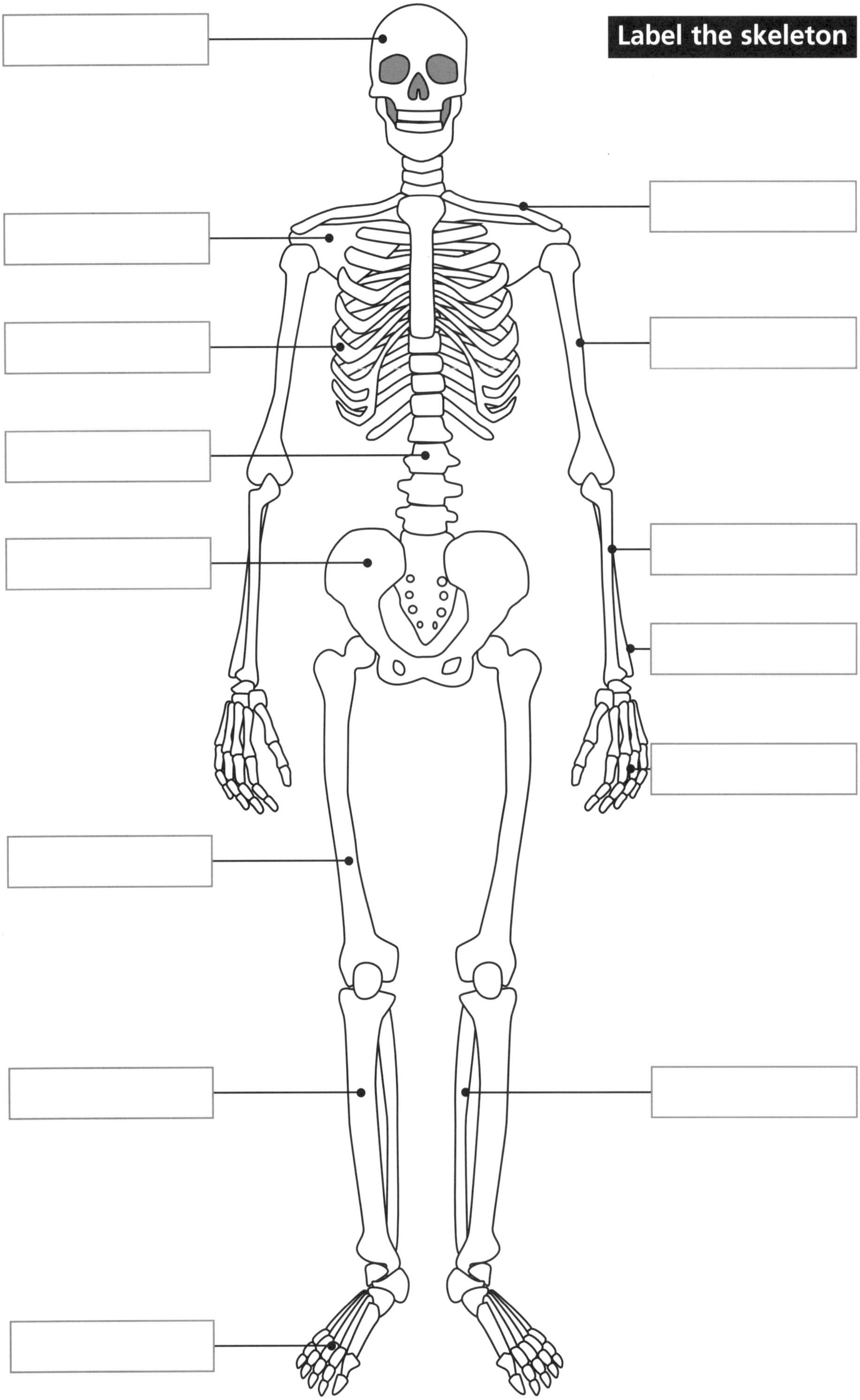

14

Label the heart

marks

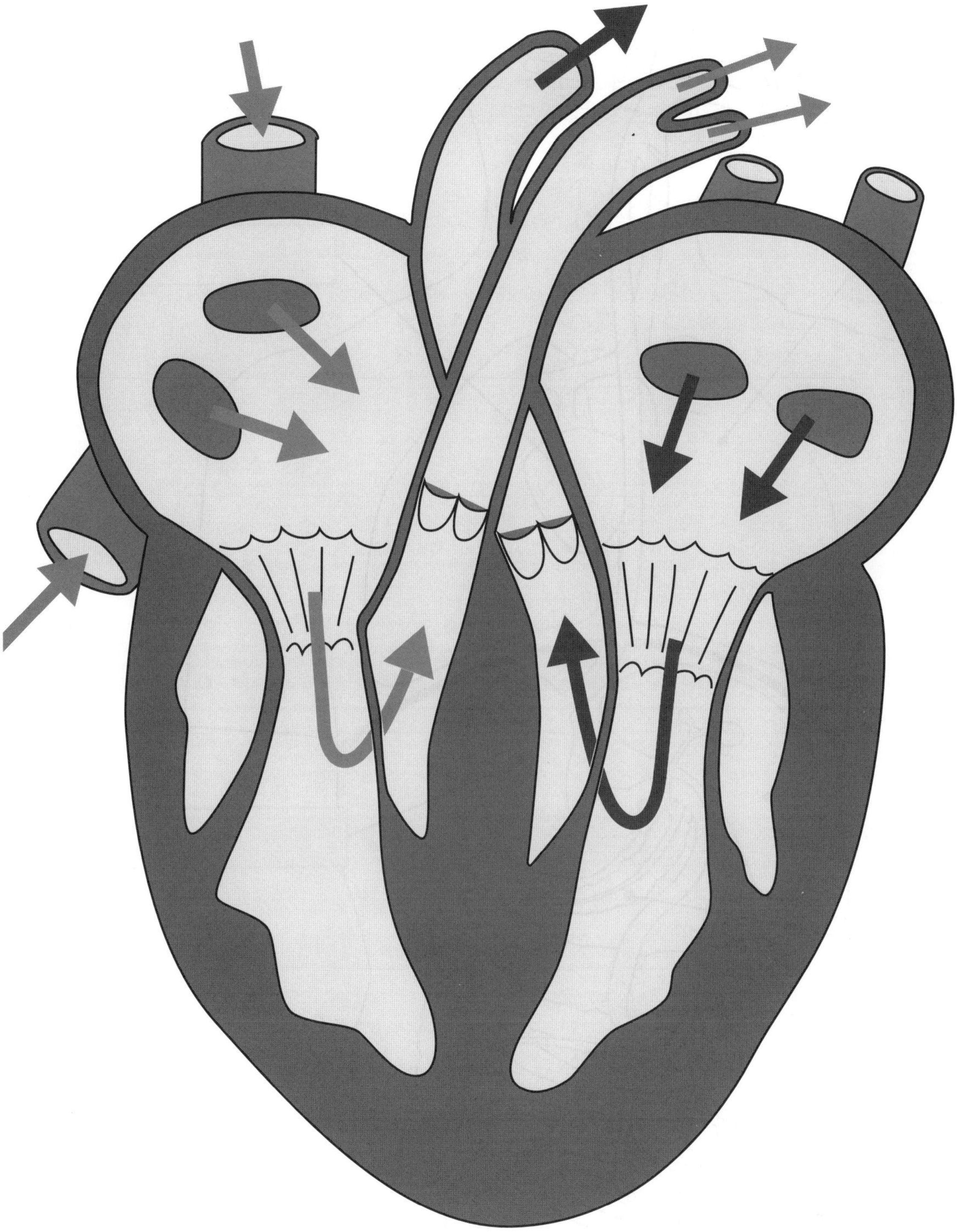

Can you describe how the heart works?

6

Letts

marks

Label the parts of the digestive system and body organs

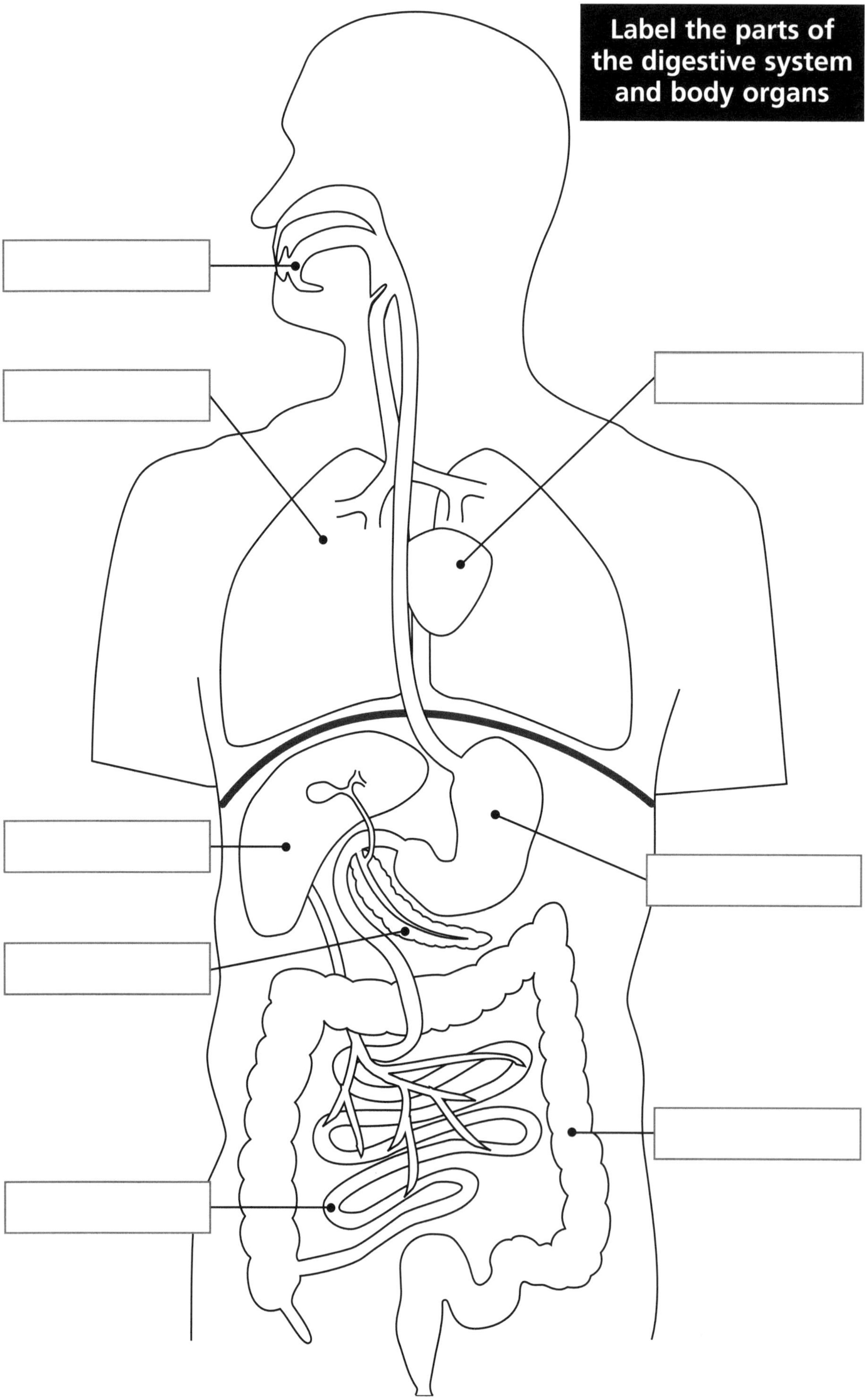

8

Letts

marks

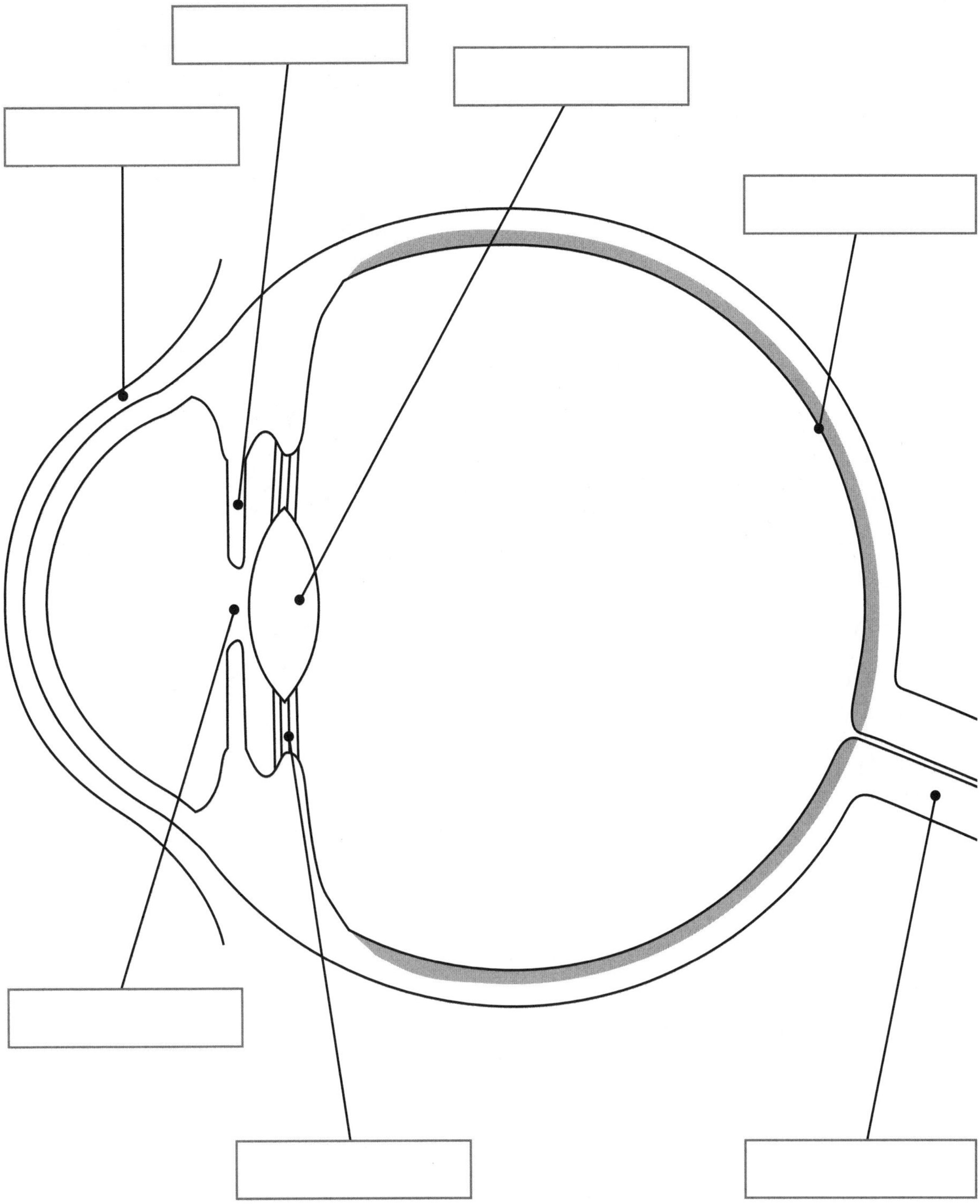

Label the parts of the human eye

7

Letts

marks

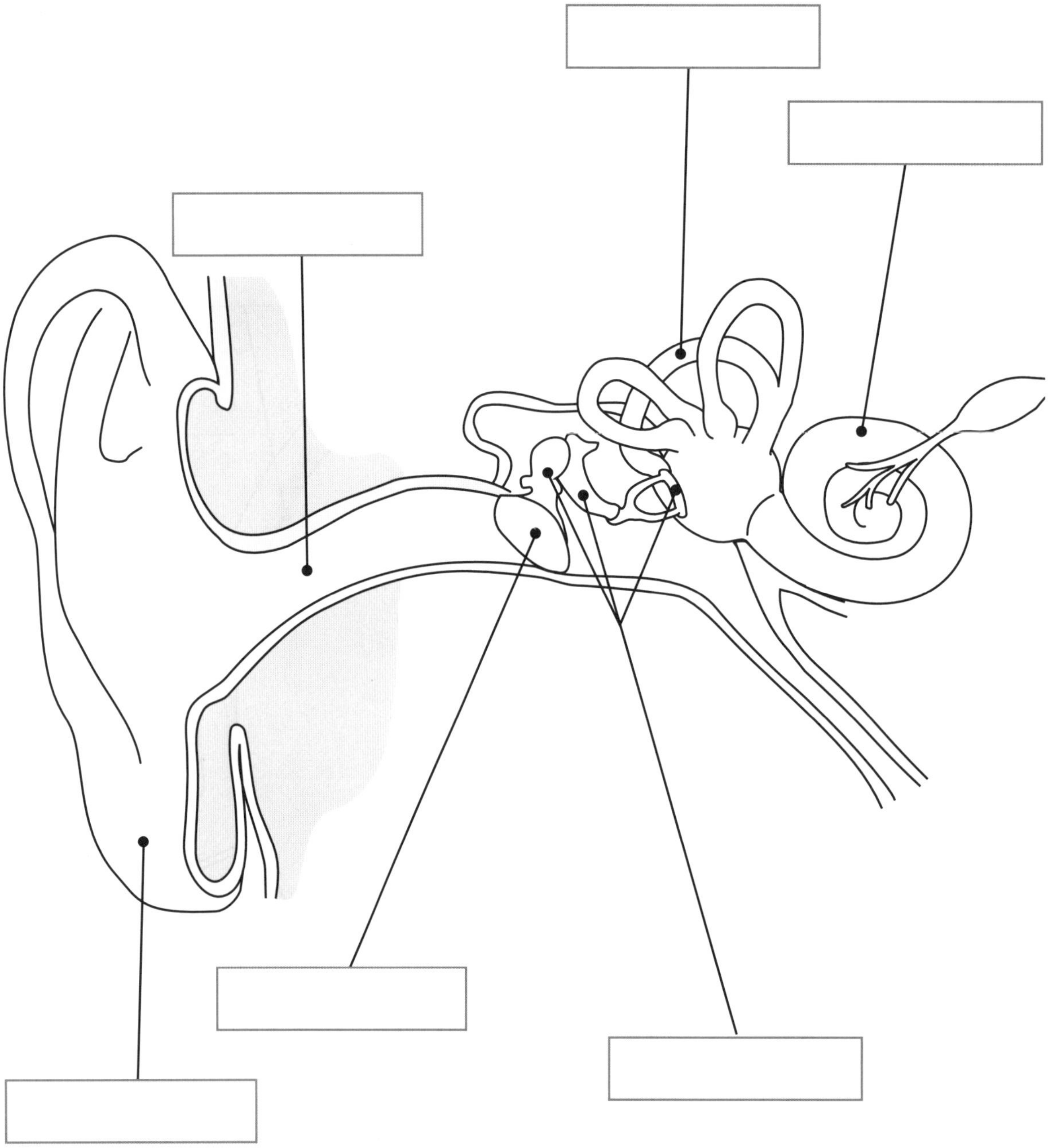

Label the parts of the human ear

6

Letts

marks

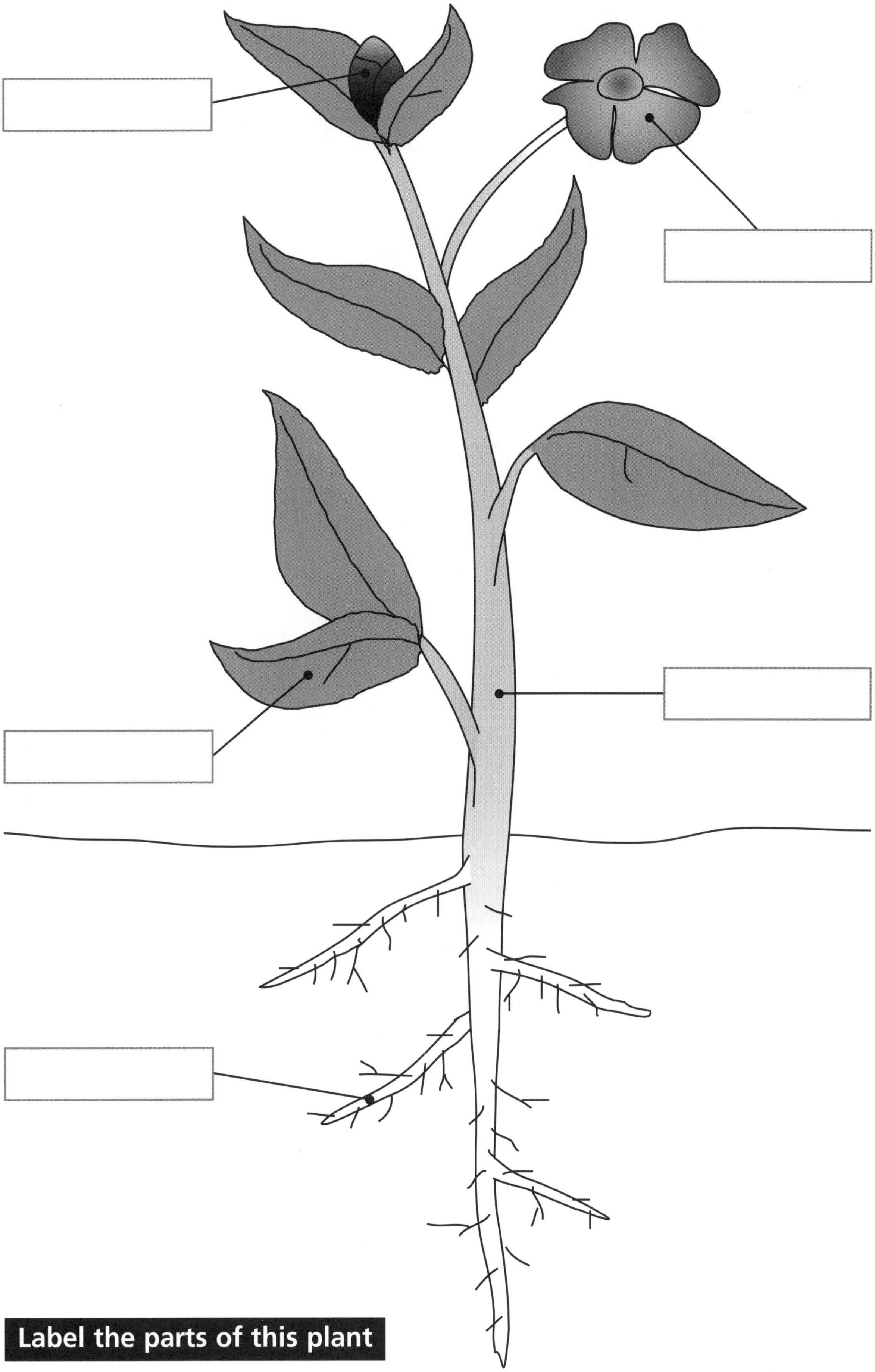

Label the parts of this plant

Draw arrows to show how water travels to all parts of the plant.

5

marks

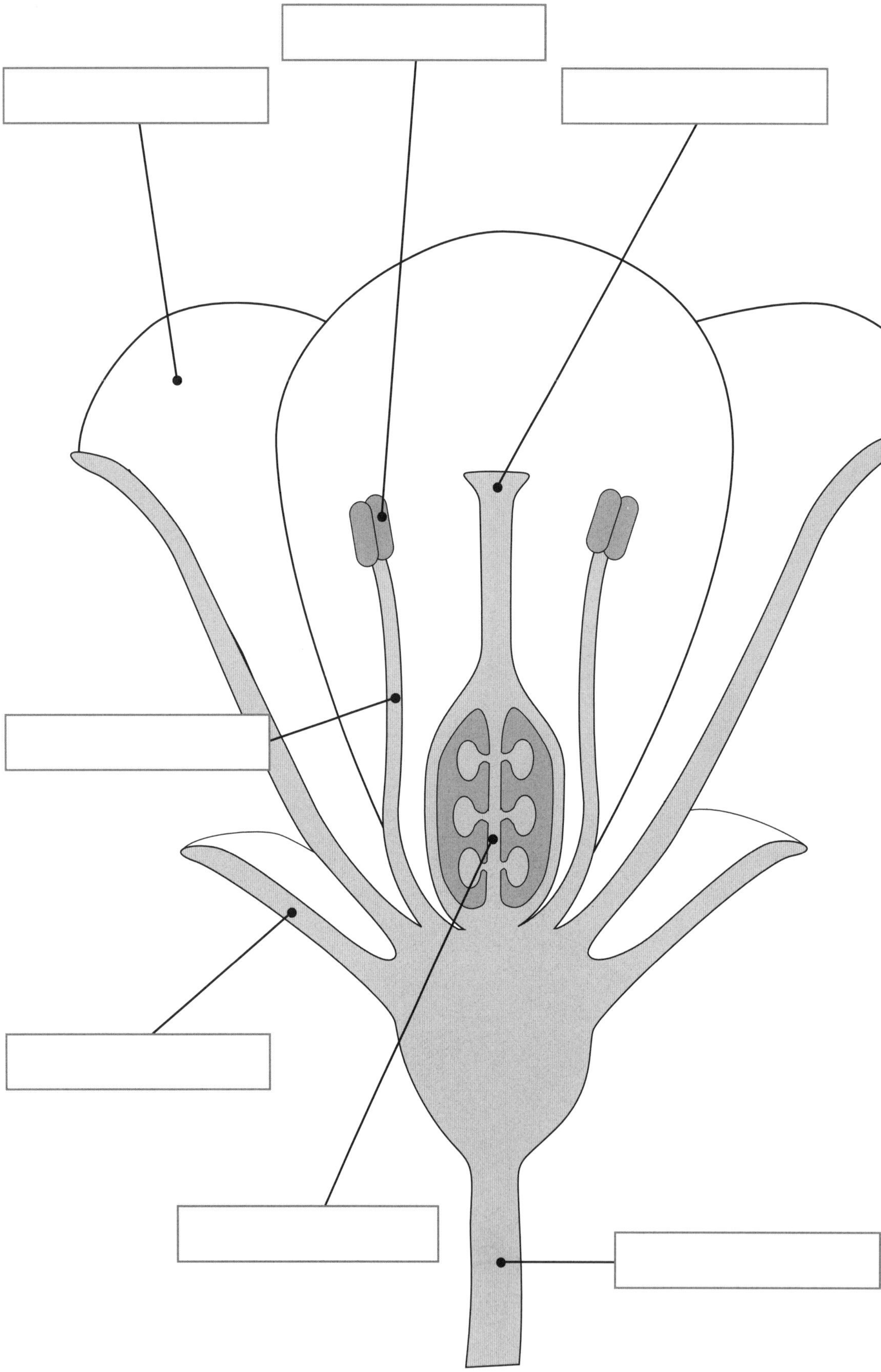

Label the parts of this flower

7

marks

Seed dispersal

Join the pictures to the correct description.

1. Some seeds have little hooks that stick to animals' fur.

2. Some seeds are eaten by birds.

3. Some seeds are buried by squirrels in a food store.

4. Some seeds are so light they can be blown by the wind.

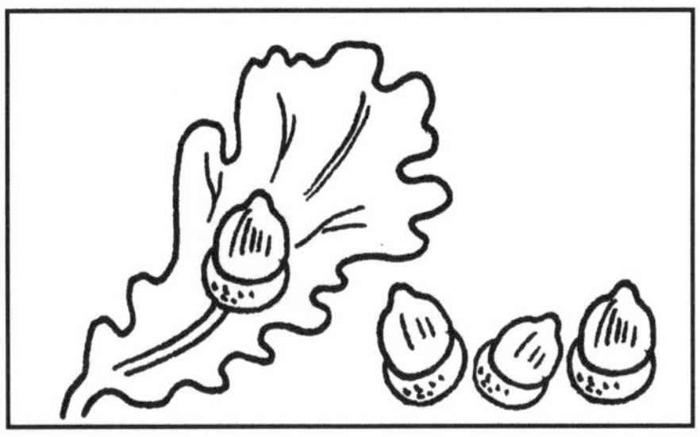

5. Some seeds grow in a pod which bursts open, flinging the seeds away.

6. Some seeds are carried away by water.

6

Letts

marks

Label the teeth. Write what each one does.

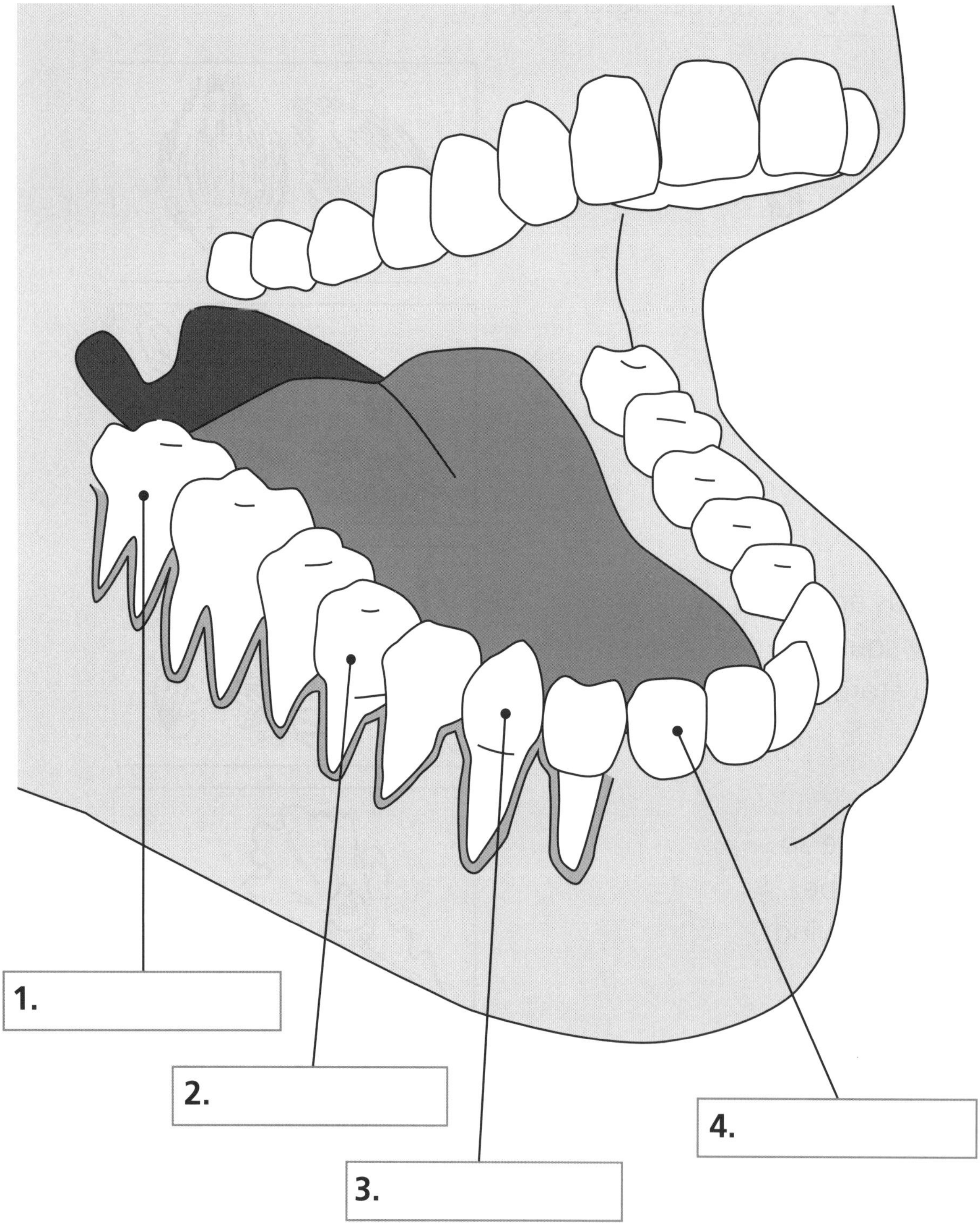

1. ______________________________

2. ______________________________

3. ______________________________

4. ______________________________

marks

Label the 4 main types of food.
Draw 2 more examples in each group.

carbohydrates

proteins fats

vitamins

12

Glossary

air resistance

the force which slows things moving through the air

amphibian

a type of animal which lives on land and water and lays its eggs in water

artery

a strong tube (blood vessel) through which blood flows away from the heart

carbon dioxide

a gas which is part of the air and used by plants to make food

carnivore

animal which eats other animals

cloud

a mass of tiny droplets of water (condensed water vapour)

condensing

turning from a gas to a liquid

crustacean

a type of animal which has jointed legs and usually has a hard outer covering, e.g. crab, woodlouse

evaporation

the change from a liquid to a gas

filtering

removing solid particles from a liquid

food chain

a list of where living things get their energy from

force

a push or pull

freezing

change from a liquid to a solid

friction

a force which slows moving things by rubbing

gravity

a pull which causes things to fall towards the Earth

herbivore

animal which eats plants

insoluble

a solid which will not dissolve

invertebrate

an animal which does not have a backbone

magnetism

a force which attracts magnetic objects

omnivore

animal which eats both plants and animals

photosynthesis

the way plants make food using sunlight, water and carbon dioxide

reptile

an animal with scales which lays leathery eggs on land

solar system

the Sun and its nine planets

Your Notes

Your Notes